BUSES IN EAST YORKSHIRE

JOHN LAW

AMBERLEY

First published 2023

Amberley Publishing
The Hill, Stroud
Gloucestershire, GL5 4EP

www.amberley-books.com

Copyright © John Law, 2023

The right of John Law to be identified as
the Author of this work has been asserted in
accordance with the Copyrights, Designs and
Patents Act 1988.

ISBN 978 1 3981 1261 2 (print)
ISBN 978 1 3981 1262 9 (ebook)

British Library Cataloguing in Publication Data.
A catalogue record for this book is available from
the British Library.

Origination by Amberley Publishing.
Printed in the UK.

Introduction

In 1974, the former East Riding of Yorkshire fell into the hands of the newly created Humberside County Council. This authority controlled local government on both sides of the Humber, and was never popular with residents of Yorkshire or Lincolnshire. Common sense eventually prevailed and Humberside was abolished in 1996. East Yorkshire was reborn! It had also expanded. The town of Goole and part of its surroundings, in the West Riding until 1974, was included in the new boundaries.

Geographically, East Yorkshire can be divided into two parts. There are the flat lands, extending from around Goole, along the Humber, through Kingston-upon-Hull to Holderness and Spurn Head. There is also an area of chalk hills, known as the Yorkshire Wolds. There is one major city: Kingston-upon-Hull (usually referred to as just 'Hull'), one of the major ports of the United Kingdom. Some of the waterborne transport comes up the Humber to the inland port of Goole. Bridlington is the main seaside resort, with the smaller coastal towns of Hornsea and Withernsea also attracting holidaymakers. Several small towns can be found inland, including Driffield, Howden, Market Weighton and Pocklington.

Horse-drawn tram operations began in the city of Hull in 1875 by the Hull Street Tramways Company. In 1889, the Drypool & Marfleet Steam Tramway Company started running. 1896 saw both of these undertakings acquired by Hull Corporation and electrification soon followed. An unusual feature of Hull's tramways was the use of centre-grooved rails – the only other major operation having this feature being Doncaster. Trams in Kingston-upon-Hull ceased running on 30 June 1945.

In 1933, Kingston-upon-Hull Corporation signed a co-ordination agreement with East Yorkshire Motor Services, which helped bring about the demise of the city's trams. Trolleybuses and motorbuses replaced them. The trolleybus system, latterly employing distinctive dual-door vehicles, lasted until 1964.

The city's motorbus fleet was seriously depleted during the bombing of the Second World War, resulting in various types of second-hand vehicles being purchased. It is said that many of these ended up as infill when the conversion of Queens Dock into a city centre garden took place. The year 1960 saw the first of many Leyland Atlanteans being bought new. Deliveries continued until 1982. A few AEC Reliance saloons were also bought new, later followed by Leyland Panthers. Later purchases included Scania Metropolitans and Dennis Dominators.

In 1986, in common with all other former municipal operators, they became an arm's-length company, with the majority shareholder being the city council. Deregulation and completion meant increasing losses and, in 1993, KHCT was sold to Cleveland Transit, based in Stockton-on-Tees. The following year Stagecoach took over all operations and today run many of the city's bus services.

The other major operator in the area was East Yorkshire Motor Services, which was formed in 1926, after the merger of two smaller companies. It later became part of the British Electric Traction Group and grew to cover virtually the entire East Riding. Various businesses were acquired, including Williamson's of Bridlington and Everingham Brothers from Pocklington.

The double-deck vehicles of EYMS were easily recognisable as the bodywork on them was built to a special profile to fit (just!) under Beverley Bar. The obstruction was later by-passed and, since the 1970s, standard buses can by used.

In 1969, EYMS passed into the ownership of the National Bus Company. Initially, a dark blue livery was adopted, in NBC style, but was quickly replaced by standard 'poppy' red. Privatisation came in 1987, with a management buy-out. Ownership later went to Mr Peter Shipp and East Yorkshire, as the company became known, continued independently until 2018. That was when the Go-Ahead Group took over. East Yorkshire today remains a 'stand-alone' business within the larger Go North East organisation.

From the 1950s until deregulation in 1986, EYMS and KHCT had a near monopoly of bus services in the old East Riding of Yorkshire. One independent managed to hang on – Connor & Graham. This company, based in the Holderness village of Easington had commenced operations in 1921 and ran a route into central Hull, as well as a couple of services around Withernsea. The business finally ceased bus services in 1993.

Deregulation meant that several independent companies commenced competing services in the Hull area. Council tendering also saw a number of smaller operators win some rural routes. Various names such as Humber Stagecoach, Appleby's and Rhodes have now all disappeared, leaving East Yorkshire Motor Services and the Stagecoach Group with a virtual monopoly.

Having said the above, there is one town where there has been – and still is – a number of different operators. Goole has always been a 'border town', where east meets west. Lincolnshire Road Car arrived via the scarcely populated flat lands from Scunthorpe. These services are today operated by Sweyne Coaches. The West Riding Automobile Company had regular buses coming in to Goole from the Pontefract direction. These are now in the hands of Arriva. Finally, the Blue Line/Reliance concern from the Doncaster area ran their buses into Goole until taken over by South Yorkshire PTE in 1979. Today there are no bus services between Thorne Moorends and Goole.

To conclude, it must be stated that the county of East Yorkshire has long been a source of great interest to bus enthusiasts and remains so to the present day.

I am grateful to the following for supplying a few photographs: Les Flint, Richard Huggins, Jim Sambrooks, Richard Simons and Peter Tuffrey.

Car No. 23, hauled by two faithful horses, enters the Temple Street depot (just off Beverley Road) for the last time, in November 1899.

The Drypool & Marfleet Steam Tramway Company employed a fleet of tram locos built in Leeds by Thomas Green & Son. This one, together with its seventy-four-seat trailer, is seen operating the Alexandra Dock to North Bridge service. The last steam tram ran in 1901. (Thanks to Peter Tuffrey for supplying these photographs)

Kingston-upon-Hull Corporation tram No. 17, built in 1899 is seen on Anlaby Road and photographed prior to 1909, when all this type had received top deck covers. Like others in the batch, it had Brill trucks and bodies capable of seating fifty-one passengers. (Peter Tuffrey Collection)

The city of Hull was cursed with an abundance of level crossings. Here, 1904-built car No. 116 waits for one of the frequent trains at by Botanic Gardens station. Trams at this spot were controlled by railway-style semaphore signals, one of which can be clearly seen at 'danger'. An intrepid cyclist has taken advantage of the stationary tram, saving his feet from touching the road surface!

One intact example of Hull's trams survived into preservation. No. 132 was found inside Cottingham Road depot on 26 August 1984. It has since been restored and can be seen in the Streetlife Museum of Transport in Hull's Old Town. (Richard Huggins)

Trolleybuses were introduced to the streets of Hull in 1937. One of a batch of ten Sunbeam F4 vehicles purchased in 1948, No. 100 (HRH 100) is seen in the city centre *c.* 1960. It was withdrawn in 1960.

Brush-bodied Sunbeam W4 No. 70 (GRH 290) in Hull city centre, with its booms down, during an enthusiasts' tour *c.* 1960.This vehicle was withdrawn in 1963.

The first of the 'Coronation' trolleybuses was delivered in 1953, followed by further batches arriving in the next two years. Among the last to be received was No. 115 (RKH 115). The dual-doored fifty-four-seat Roe bodywork is on a Sunbeam MF2B chassis. It is seen, again on a photo stop during an enthusiasts' special, having just crossed the River Hull by means of the Drypool Bridge.

Another view of 'Coronation' trolleybus No. 115 on tour, this time showing the offside and its double staircase. The location is in the yard of Holderness Road depot towards the very end of the trolleybus operations.

On the same occasion as the top photograph, a row of withdrawn trolleybuses is a sad sight at Holderness Road. Several participants of the tour take notes and pay their last respects.

Moving on to the motorbus fleet, here we have KHCT No. 199 (GKH 380) at Holderness Road depot. This 1942-built AEC Regent originally carried a Northern Counties 'utility' body, which was replaced in 1950 by the fifty-six-seat version seen here, built by Weymann in 1937.

Photographed inside Holderness Road depot towards the end of its life is No. 236 (GRH 381). A 1945-built Guy Arab II, it has a fifty-six-seat Massey body, built to 'utility' standards. It was withdrawn in 1962.

Another wartime (1944) Guy Arab II, No. 216 (GRH 131), looks splendid inside Cottingham Road depot on 22 August 1962. It had been fitted with a 1937-built Weymann body that had been previously carried by a Daimler COG5. Final withdrawal came in 1963. (Les Flint)

The early post war years saw various batches of AEC Regents being delivered. No. 299 (KAT 299) was a Mark III version, new in 1949. Like most of the others, it was fitted with a fifty-eight-seat Weymann body. It is seen alongside the earliest of many Leyland Atlantean PDR1/1 types, No. 347 (2347 AT). Both are waiting at traffic lights in Hull city centre on 22 August 1962. (Les Flint)

The year 1962 was when KHCT took delivery of its first batch of Leyland PDR1/1 Atlanteans. Arriving a year later was 379 (3379 RH), with Roe bodywork seating seventy-five passengers. It is seen here, renumbered as 179, in its old-style livery at Ferensway in central Hull, 1975.

KHCT received various batches of Leyland Atlanteans over the years, with the last ones coming in 1975. No. 253 (PRH 253G) was new in 1969 and was of PDR1A/1 specification, again with Roe bodywork, though featuring a one-piece windscreen. It is seen in the latest livery of the time outside Ferensway bus station in 1980.

In 1960, Hull's municipal fleet received five Weymann B39D-bodied AEC Reliances to add to a few earlier saloons of a similar type. Originally numbered 169, but seen in 1973 as No. 69 (5169 KH) resting in the yard beside Hull Paragon railway station.

For single-deck requirements, KHCT turned to the Leyland Panther PSUR1/1, with deliveries commencing in 1964. All had dual-doored Roe bodies. One of the last to arrive, No. 180 (GAT 180D), new in 1966, is seen renumbered as 80 inside the depot, adjacent to Ferensway bus station in 1980.

In 1975, the first of Hull's Metropolitan double-deck buses was delivered. A total of thirty were received. Numerically the last, No. 430 (WKH 430S), a seventy-four-seat vehicle, was photographed leaving the city centre depot in 1980. Further Metropolitans appeared in 1983, bought second-hand from Merseyside.

Five unusual Ford AO609 minibuses, with Tricentrol twenty-three-seat bodies were purchased in 1976. Among the specialised duties for these was the short route 50, linking the bus/rail stations with Corporation Pier, connecting with the Humber Ferry to New Holland. No. 13 (MAT 13P) is seen beside the Humber in 1977. The need for this service vanished in 1981 when the Humber Bridge opened, and this batch of buses was withdrawn in that year.

The year 1980 saw fifteen MCW Metrobus double-deck vehicles, each seating seventy-three passengers. Almost new at the time, the last in the batch, No. 515 (LAT 515V), is seen at Boothferry Park, Hull, about to take part in the East Coast Run to Bridlington.

Despite the influx of MCW products, more Leyland Atlanteans were bought in 1982. Among them was No. 381 (WAG 381X), an AN68C/1R with seventy-four-seat Roe bodywork. It was photographed during a day out in Bridlington in the year of its purchase.

A 'one-off' in the KHCT fleet was No. 60 (B60 WKH), a twenty-four-seat Leyland National 2, fitted with a wheelchair lift. Intended for special duties, it is seen in Hull in mid-1986.

Lettered as a 'Royale' vehicle, No. 601 (D601 MKH) was the first of fifteen Iveco/Fiat 49.10 minibuses, fitted with twenty-five-seat Robin Hood bodywork. Almost new when photographed in early 1987, it is seen outside Cottingham Road depot.

Dennis Dominators began to appear in the Hull fleet as early as 1984, but three, numbered 111 to 113, were special, as their bodies, built by East Lancs, were fitted out with seventy-one coach seats. Seen in the 'Kingstonian' coach livery, 111 (C111 CAT) was photographed as it departed from its city starting point on a rally to Bridlington in 1986, when almost brand new.

Despite plenty of Dennis Dominators being delivered, KHCT found it necessary to purchase some second-hand buses. These included eight Leyland Atlantean PDR2/1 double-deckers, bought from West Yorkshire PTE in 1986. All had been new to Bradford Corporation. 464 (TKU 464K), with dual-doored Alexander bodywork, is seen parked near Ferensway in 1986. (Richard Simons)

The year 1988 saw the delivery of six unusual buses into the Hull fleet. One of them was photographed in Ferensway bus station in 1989. No. 706 (F706 CAG) is an East Lancs-bodied Scania N112CRB with forty-nine dual-purpose seats. It looks very smart in the latest livery of the time.

More Scania/East Lancs vehicles were to appear in 1989 and 1990, but these were more conventional for Hull. Numbers 801 to 816 were of Scania N113DRB types with double-deck bodies seating eighty-eight passengers. Our example is No. 804 (G804 JRH), seen under the roof of Ferensway bus station in the spring of 1990.

Citilink was a post deregulation operator that was taken over by KHCT in 1989. The new owners relaunched the operation using older Leyland Atlanteans from the main fleet. Here in its new guise is No. C1 (WRH 281J). The vehicle is of type PDR1/1, with Roe bodywork, previously No. 281 in the Hull fleet. It was photographed near Ferensway in the summer of 1989. The Citilink services were absorbed into the main operations in 1992.

In December 1993, fifty-two per cent of KHCT's holding was sold to Cleveland Transit and a new livery was introduced to reflect the change. Seen in its new colours, alongside Paragon station, is No. 136 (E136 SAT), a 1987-built Dennis Dominator with an East Lancs body. The photograph was taken in mid-1994.

Transferred in from the associated Cleveland Transit fleet was Leyland Atlantean PDR1A/1 No. 946 (SDC 146H), photographed in Hull in summer 1994. It had been delivered to Teesside in 1970 but had received a new Northern Counties body in 1984. After service in Hull, it was converted to open-top and exported.

East Lancs-bodied Dennis Dominator No. 132 (E132 SAT) was painted in a special livery to wear on duties between central Hull and King George Dock, in connection with North Sea Ferries. On 10 June 1995, it was photographed among the maritime warehouses awaiting the journey into the city. (Richard Huggins)

In 1995, Hull received a batch of forty-eight-seat Volvo B10M-55 saloons, bodied by Northern Counties. One of them, No. 715 (M715 KRH) was photographed on an overcast day in mid-1995 as it arrived at the rally site in Bridlington, having just completed the East Coast Run.

Though Cleveland Transit and its associated acquisitions had been bought by Stagecoach Holdings in 1994, it was not until 1995 that visible evidence began to appear on the buses. MCW Metrobus 524 (SAG 524W) is seen with its new logos in central Hull around that time.

In 1988, Hull had received a batch of five East Lancs-bodied Scania N112CRB saloons, each with forty-nine dual-purpose seats. No. 704 (F704 BAT) is seen under the roof of Ferensway bus station in Hull, in Stagecoach stripes, December 1996.

Delivered to Stagecoach subsidiary Cleveland Transit were three articulated Volvo B10MA-55 coaches. These unusual vehicles each had seventy-two-seat Jonckheere bodies. They were used, as can be deduced from the destination blind and side lettering, on express services to Sheffield – from both sides of the Humber. No. 97 (T97 JHN) was photographed arriving at Ferensway, Hull, in mid-1999, almost brand new at the time. These services did not last very long.

No. 927 (E927 KYR) in the Stagecoach Hull fleet had been new to London Transport's Bexleybus subsidiary in 1987. This Northern Counties-bodied Leyland Olympian was photographed at Ferensway bus station in the summer of 2000. Stagecoach sold it in 2003 and it ended up with a Dorset operator, Shamrock Buses of Poole.

Looking very much like a typical Stagecoach vehicle, No. 32080 (M64 VJO) had been delivered as fleet number 3018 with Thames Transit in the Oxford area. It later moved to the East London operations of Stagecoach. Originally a dual-doored Dennis Dart with Plaxton Pointer bodywork it is seen in central Hull on 11 July 2006, after conversion to single-door.

The latest Stagecoach colour scheme had recently been applied to 22773 (FX09 DCF), photographed as it leaves Hull's new interchange, alongside Paragon railway station on 9 June 2021. This MAN 18.240 with an Alexander Dennis B46F body had been new in March 2009.

As a special treat for the residents of Kingston-upon-Hull, Stagecoach repainted this Alexander-bodied Dennis Trident as the '110th Anniversary Bus'. 18435 (YN06 LMM) looks rather grand in the old livery of KHCT as it departs from Hull Interchange on 6 September 2009.

We now move on and take a look at East Yorkshire Motor Services (EYMS) with their distinctive 'Beverley Bar' profiles, designed to fit – just – through that gateway. Pictured here, in central Hull, is No. 399 (GKH 531), a 1943 Guy Arab I. It had originally carried a Brush 'utility' body, but had been rebodied by Roe in 1953. 399 lasted in service until 1961.

1956 saw the delivery of fifteen AEC Regent V double-deck buses, each fitted with fifty-six-seat Willowbrook bodywork, including platform doors. No. 643's 'Beverley Bar' profile is shown to good advantage as it pauses in Bridlington bus station in August 1963. 643 (VKH 43) was the first of the batch to be withdrawn, in 1970. (Les Flint)

One of the 1956 batch of Willowbrook-bodied AEC Regent V types has survived and is still with EYMS as a 'heritage' vehicle, used on special duties. No. 644 (VKH 44) was photographed on a private hire duty outside the Eagle pub in Skerne, a small village south of Driffield, in spring 1998. While 644 is still with us, the totally unspoilt Eagle sadly closed in 2004.

No book depicting buses in East Yorkshire would be complete without a photograph of a vehicle negotiating the Beverley Bar, a famous fifteenth-century gate separating North Bar Without and North Bar Within. Even double-deck buses designed to pass under low bridges, such as this AEC Bridgemaster, had to have the bodywork profile adopted for this obstacle. New in 1961, No. 715 (4715 AT) had Park Royal H48/28RD bodywork. Double-deck buses ceased operating through the bar after the opening of a new road in 1970. Photograph taken 22 August 1962. (Les Flint)

EYMS No. 756 (3756 RH) was another AEC Bridgemaster, delivered in 1963. Again, Park Royal provided the body, seating seventy-two passengers, but this time with a forward entrance. It was photographed in the parking area beside Paragon station in Hull, not long before being withdrawn in 1975.

1964 saw the delivery of the first batch of AEC Renowns to EYMS. One of the first to arrive was No. 760 (9760 RH). Park Royal seventy-five-seat bodywork is carried. It is still wearing the dark blue National Bus Company livery, as is the ex-Tynemouth & District Daimler Fleetline alongside. Other vehicles are painted into NBC red. 756 was withdrawn in 1975.

More Park Royal-bodied AEC Renowns were delivered to EYMS in 1965, this time just seating seventy passengers. One of them, No. 784 (CKH 784C), waits for its next duty outside the pub adjoining Ferensway bus station in Hull, on a foul day in 1976. It was not withdrawn until 1979. More AEC Renowns arrived in 1966, with the last one going in 1980.

The final double-deck buses to be built to the 'Beverley Bar' design were Daimler Fleetlines. Numerically the first to be delivered, in 1967, was No. 825 (MAT 825F), with sixty-eight-seat Park Royal bodywork. It is seen here, in central Hull, still in its pre-NBC livery, in July 1972. It survived until withdrawal in 1980.

Now in full NBC red livery at Hull in mid-1980 is another Park Royal-bodied Daimler Fleetline, No. 857 (NKH 87F). This bus was finally withdrawn in 1988, marking the end of 'Beverley Bar' buses in the main fleet.

In 1968, EYMS took delivery of eight Leyland PSURC1/1 Panther Cubs with forty-five-seat Marshall bodies. One of them, No. 840 (PKH 840G), is seen beside Paragon station in Hull, c. 1975. Along with most of the batch, 840 was withdrawn in 1979.

As well as the Panther Cubs, EYMS also bought several Leyland Panther single-deckers. One delivered in 1968, No. 847 (MAT 847F), of PSUR1/2RT specification, with dual-purpose forty-nine-seat Marshall bodywork, was found in Hull in mid-1980.

No 850 in the EYMS fleet, registered MRH 850F, was one of three Leyland PSUR1/2RT Panthers to full coaching standards, carrying a forty-four-seat Plaxton body. It is about to embark on an excursion from Hull in 1977.

EYMS did not acquire many second-hand vehicles in NBC days, but an exception was the purchase of several ex-Tynemouth & District Daimler Fleetlines. One of them, No. 907 (DFT 290E), with seventy-five-seat Alexander bodywork was photographed in Hull in 1977.

Sister vehicle 900 (AFT 783C) was later converted to open-top, given the name *Belvedere Star* and put into summer use in Bridlington, where it is seen on a working to Sewerby in 1979.

Another ex-Tynemouth & District Daimler Fleetline, this time with a Metro-Cammell H44/31F body, is seen in the sun in Bridlington bus station in 1979. No. 912 (HFT 368), built in 1963, had been acquired in 1972. It lasted in EYMS service until 1980.

In 1975, EYMS purchased five Leyland Leopard coaches, with Alexander forty-nine-seat Y-type bodywork. No. 157 (DDB 157C) came from National Travel (North West) but had been new to North Western Road Car Company. It was photographed in Hull in 1977 and withdrawn two years later.

1971 saw the delivery of more Daimler Fleetlines, this time with seventy-five-seat Alexander bodies. One example, No. 891 (WKH 891J) was found in Beverley in August 1984.

Some Leyland PDR1/3 Atlanteans were also purchased by EYMS in 1971. Alexander bodywork was fitted, this time with seventy-three seats. No. 898 (AAT 398K) was photographed in Hull, almost new, in traditional colours.

Another of the 1971-built Atlanteans, No. 895 (AAT 395K) is seen parked up in Hull in 1980, painted in standard NBC red. All of this batch were withdrawn in 1986.

The EYMS single-deck fleet must not be forgotten. In 1969, the company purchased seven dual-purpose Leyland Leopards, with Marshall bodies, each seating forty-nine passengers. No. 881 (RKH 881G) was photographed in Bridlington bus station in 1980. This vehicle went out of service a year later.

The last of the 'non-standard' NBC double-deckers for EYMS was a batch of fifteen Park Royal-bodied Leyland Atlantean AN68/1R types, each seating seventy-three passengers. Two of them were photographed, not long after delivery in 1974, in Hull, these being 947 (PAT 947M) and 946 (PAT 946M).

Looking very smart in NBC red livery is another of the same delivery, No. 950 (PAT 950M), seen between duties in Hull in 1980. This vehicle had a decent spell in the EYMS fleet, not being withdrawn until 1993.

No. 952 (originally registered PAT 952M), another of the Park Royal-bodied Leyland Atlanteans, was refurbished in 1989 and given a new registration, TIJ 952, a year later. In its new guise, it was captured on film arriving at Ferensway, Hull, in the summer of 1994. It was to continue in service for another two years.

As well as the Atlanteans, EYMS also standardised on the Bristol VR types for its double-deck requirements. The first ones were delivered in 1973, in the dark blue NBC livery. No. 929 (DKH 929L), an ECW-bodied VRTSL/6G is seen in Hull in the mid-1970s.

The National Bus Company soon got rid of non-standard colour schemes and the buses of EYMS soon appeared in the ubiquitous 'poppy red' paintwork, as seen applied to Bristol VR/ECW seventy-seat vehicles 926 and 928 (DKH 926/8L) parked up in Hull. This first batch of such vehicles were all withdrawn in 1988.

More Bristol VRTSL/6G types, with ECW bodywork seating seventy passengers appeared in the EYMS fleet in 1974. One of them, No. 938 (GAG 45N) was found running alongside the beach in Hornsea, August 1984.

It would be fair to say that EYMS did not show a great liking for the Leyland National, even though it was a standard vehicle for National Bus Company subsidiaries. The first order, delivered in 1975, was for just five buses. Here is one of that batch, No. 167 (NRH 167P), seen in Hull in the early 1980s.

Like 167 (above), No. 169 (RAG 169R) was another forty-nine-seated Leyland National. It was later given a wheelchair lift and received just twenty-five dual-purpose seats. In such configuration, it was photographed in Hull in 1986. It remained in service until 1996.

Unusually, the year 1976 saw the delivery of five Ford R1014 saloons, with forty-three-seat Duple bus bodies. One of these, No. 174 (NRH 174P), was photographed in Beverley bus station sometime around 1978. All had been withdrawn by 1981.

Other deliveries in 1976 included the later type Bristol double-deckers, the VRT/SL3/501 types. Here is an example, No. 961 (RKH 961R), seen in Hull in 1983, decorated in National Holidays advertising livery. The standard ECW body is carried, seating seventy-four passengers.

The coaching fleet of EYMS consisted mainly of Leyland Leopards in the 1970s. An unusual second-hand purchase was that of No. 196 (KGJ 475K), with Plaxton coachwork. It had been new to fellow NBC subsidiary Samuelsons of London, though it had latterly been employed by United Automobile Services. Sometime around 1981, it was photographed in Bridlington.

In 1979, six more Leyland Leopard coaches arrived, all with forty-nine-seat Plaxton Supreme coachwork. Preparing to depart on a National Express run to Wolverhampton, No. 190 (GKH 190T) is seen in Hull in 1980.

This photo clearly shows the two types of Bristol VR buses in the EYMS fleet, with 1979-built examples 504 (left) and 508 (right, with 928 in the middle, built in 1973. The location is the yard by Ferensway bus station in Hull and the date is sometime in 1980.

Another of the 1979 batch of seventy-four-seat ECW-bodied Bristol VRT/SL3/501 types, No. 502 (JKH 502V). It is seen outside Bridlington depot in May 1984.

Painted in a version of the old EYMS colours, No. 519 (PAG 519W) was photographed in Hornsea in May 1984. New to the company in 1980, it is of type VRT/SL3/6LXB. Further Bristol VR types continued to be delivered until 1981. 519 was one of the last to be withdrawn, in 2004.

After the opening of the Humber Bridge in 1981, EYMS took delivery in 1983 of three Leyland Olympians with ECW dual-purpose bodies, seating seventy passengers. Three more followed in 1985, including No. 533 (B533 WAT), this time with seventy-two seats. It was photographed in a special blue colour scheme in Hull, having just arrived on route 350 in 1985.

The last of the Leyland Leopard coaches delivered new to EYMS were received in 1981. Some had Duple bodies, but No. 206 (XAG 206X) and a sister had coachwork by Willowbrook, seating forty-nine passengers. It is seen with a light load in Hull in 1986, a year before withdrawal.

Four Leyland Tiger coaches appeared in 1983. All carried Plaxton Paramount bodies, with No. 3 (GRH 3Y) having seats for fifty-five passengers. It was photographed arriving at Ferensway, Hull, when about a year old. Departure from the fleet came in 1987.

Though the Leyland National did not find popularity in the EYMS fleet, some of the B-type versions were purchased. These did not feature the rear-mounted roof pod. Here is No. 180 (BRH 180T), a forty-one-seat vehicle, passing the old lighthouse in Flamborough in May 1984. The tower was built in 1674 and is the earliest lighthouse still in existence in the UK.

With deregulation and privatisation looming, the National Bus Company began to allow variations from its corporate colour scheme. In mid-1987, Leyland National 169 (RAG 169R) was photographed on a dull day in Hull. It is seen wearing the new style of red and white and the latest version of the fleet name.

No. 919 on the EYMS books, registered ATA 557L, entered the fleet in 1986, having previously operated with Devon General. The ECW-bodied Bristol VRTSL/6G is seen in its new colours at Anlaby Road depot in Hull in the summer of 1987.

The minibus era began in 1985 with EYMS. One of the first to arrive was No. 310 (C310 DRH), a sixteen-seat Ford Transit converted to bus use by Carlyle. It was found in Beverley bus station in autumn 1987. It was withdrawn the following year.

More second-hand purchases arrived towards the end of the 1980s. One such, registered KSU 876P, a Leyland Atlantean AN68A/1R with Alexander bodywork, began life with Greater Glasgow PTE. It later passed through the hands of London Country before becoming No. 876 in the EYMS fleet. As such, it was photographed outside Anlaby Road depot, Hull, in 1991.

EYMS No. 18 was a MCW Metroliner double-deck coach, originally registered C118 FKH. It was later rebadged as 665 EYL. Here it is, in Ferensway bus station, Hull, in the summer of 1994. On disposal to Ensign (Dealer) it was again reregistered, as C593 JAT, and converted to open-top.

Like many other operators, EYMS purchased several AEC Routemasters from London Buses, including former RM798 (WLT 798). Given the fleet number of 802 it looks splendid in the retro-style blue livery, laying over in Hull in summer 1989.

Another vehicle to gain a repaint into an old colour scheme was coach No. 190, a 1979-built Leyland Leopard/Plaxton combination. Originally registered GKH 190T, it is seen here as 8225 KH in the old primrose and blue coaching colours at Anlaby Road depot in March 1987.

Painted in a special version of the coach livery, No. 545 (B109 LPH) was photographed on Anlaby Road in Hull on 20 May 1991. This coach-seated Leyland Olympian with sleek bodywork by ECW had been new to London Country with whom it bore the number LRC9. (Richard Huggins)

In similar paintwork, open-topper No. 903 (931 GTA), named *Bridlington Star*, is seen in Flamborough on a beautiful August day in 1984. Another second-hand purchase, this Leyland Atlantean PDR1/1 with a Metro-Cammell body had been received by Devon General in 1961.

This Leyland Atlantean PDR1A/1, registered SXG 50H, had been new to Teesside in 1970, carrying a Northern Counties body. It had been rebodied, again by Northern Counties, in 1984. It later passed to EYMS and was photographed in Hull as fleet No. 918, before being reregistered as NJI 1251. (Richard Simons)

A sister vehicle from the Teesside fleet, EYMS No. 933 (SDC 143H). It is posed for the camera outside Anlaby Road depot in Hull in 1994. It would later receive the registration FBZ 2933.

One of only two such vehicles in the fleet, EYMS No. 15 (C115 DRH) was a Leyland Royal Tiger integral coach, originally seating forty-seven passengers. Delivered in 1985, it is seen in Bridlington in the following year. Withdrawal came in 1992.

East Yorkshire Motor Services was not immune to the minibus craze of the late 1980s, though it had very few of the tiny Ford Transits and things of that ilk. More suitable for stage carriage work was the Mercedes 609D, such as this twenty-four-seat example, bodied by PMT. Numbered 341 in the EYMS fleet, E101 XVM had been new to a Manchester firm, Finglands, that had sold out to EYMS in 1992. Seen in Hull in mid-1994.

It is a misty day in December 1992 and Leyland National 156 (LPR 936P) rests beside Paragon station in Hull. Though it had been new to Hants & Dorset in 1976, EYMS had acquired it with the takeover of Rhodes of Waune.

A one-off in the EYMS fleet was No. 261 (L261 AKH). It is seen in Hull in mid-1994 when only a couple of months old. It is a Volvo B6-50 with forty-seat Northern Counties bodywork.

In 1986, the Scarborough operations of United Automobile Services were transferred to EYMS, including a good number of vehicles. These included a batch of Mercedes L608D minibuses, with Reeve Burgess twenty-seat coachwork. Transferred to Hull, one of these, No. 411 (C411 VVN), was photographed in the city in mid-1994.

Another Mercedes minibus in the EYMS fleet, No. 459 (T459 JRH). Plaxton Beaver twenty-seven-seat bodywork is fitted on a O814D frame. It is seen in the 1990s livery in Hull in 2000.

EYMS bought a pair of twenty-five-seat Reebur-bodied Fiat/Iveco 49.10 for operating the Goole town service. One of them, 447 (H447 YKH), was photographed in Goole town centre in June 1994, wearing a non-standard colour scheme.

Another one-off, this DAF/Optare Spectra, a seventy-one-seat bus, seen on a terrible day in Hull in January 1993. No. 571, registered A1 EYD, had been new in the previous year.

Originally registered YPD 123 Y, EYMS No. 28 (OJI 7078), a Duple-bodied Leyland Tiger coach, had commenced operations with London Country on Green Line duties in 1983. It is seen in EYMS days leaving Driffield depot in April 1998. (Richards Simons)

Another second-hand vehicle with EYMS, No. 797 (HWJ 932W) is a Bristol VRT/SL3/501 with a standard ECW body. It had been purchased from Yorkshire Traction and ran in those colours for a while. This photograph shows it after being repainted into EYMS's red livery at Hull in the summer of 1994.

1996 and 1997 saw EYMS buy a good amount of Optare-bodied Mercedes O405 saloons. One of the earliest, delivered in June 1996 as a forty-nine-seater, No. 267 (N267 KAG) is seen in Ferensway bus station, Hull, in the summer of 1996.

The new livery soon began to be applied to most vehicles as the twenty-first century arrived. In Bridlington on 20 September 2006 is the only Volvo B6-50/Northern Counties saloon in the fleet, No. 261 (L261 AKH). An earlier photo of it appears on page 51.

A couple more of the Mercedes O814D type minibuses were delivered to EYMS in March 2002. One of them, No. 418 (YX51 MUO), was found in Bridlington bus station on 20 September 2006 operating a local service.

1995 saw the purchase by EYMS of a sizeable batch of Volvo Olympian double-deck buses, six of which had seventy-two-seat Northern Counties bodywork. This one, 588 (N588 BRH), was photographed in Hull in December 1996, alongside another Olympian, No. 591 (N591 BRH), carrying an Alexander Royale body.

An earlier Olympian, this time manufactured by Leyland, with a Northern Counties body is seen in Bridlington bus station on 20 September 2006. No.572 (K572 RRH) was the first of a dozen such vehicles, though this one was fitted out with seventy-eight coach-type seats.

No. 658 (W658 WKH) in the EYMS fleet was one of the first low-floor double-deck buses, introduced in 2000. This Volvo B7TL, bodied by Plaxton, was photographed in Hull when almost new. Only two of these particular vehicles were purchased, but, of course, plenty more low-floor buses followed.

The first low-floor single-deck vehicles arrived with EYMS in 1996 and a small batch of Optare Excel forty-five-seat saloons arrived in December and the January of 1997. No. 276 (P276 NRH) has been captured on film in Hull, spring 1998.

More low-floor buses arrived later, including ten Alexander-bodied Volvo B10BLE saloons in 2000. One of these forty-four-seat vehicles, No. 312 (W412 JAT) is seen in the centre of Hessle in mid-2002.

EYMS 461 (W461 UAG) was one of many little Dennis Dart SLF types to enter the fleet from 1999 onwards. This particular one, a Plaxton-bodied twenty-nine-seat bus, was photographed in Hull city centre on 11 July 2006.

Similar No. 491 (YY52 KXJ) was delivered in September 2002 and was found on a town service in Bridlington bus station on 20 June 2006.

January 2005 saw the arrival of five Volvo B7RLE saloons, with forty-four-seat bodies by Wrights of Ballymena. Dedicated to 'Park & Ride' duties, No. 339 (YX54 FWM) was photographed in central Hull on 11 July 2006.

More Volvo B7RLE vehicles were purchased in 2010. Capable of seating forty-five passengers inside Wright bodywork, No. 370 (YX10 EYV) is seen in Hull on 19 August 2010.

The Enterprise Plasma/Plaxton Primo single-deck bus did not find favour with many operators, but EYMS did buy a batch of six. Seating twenty-eight passengers, these vehicles were used on the more lightly patronised services. On such a duty, in Bridlington bus station is No. 497 (YX06 HVK), photographed on 20 September 2006. This vehicle later saw service with PCL Travel in Northumberland.

Another of the Plaxton Primo saloons, No. 501 (YX06 HVO) is seen on service in Hull on 19 August 2010. The unusual single-leaf door arrangement is shown to good effect.

With the 2018 takeover by the Go Ahead Group, a smart new livery was introduced and is seen applied to thirty-nine-seat saloon No. 379 (YX14 RXF) passing the City Hall in Hull on 10 June 2021. One of many Alexander Dennis Enviro E20D types to enter the fleet, this one coming in June 2014.

An earlier style of Alexander Dennis Enviro design is applied to EYMS 271 (YX56 DZJ), seen as it departs from Hull Interchange on 9 June 2021. It was one of five that had been bought for an associated business, that of Finglands, Manchester.

As late as 2021, many EYMS buses were still wearing the older livery. Looking quite smart on 7 June was No. 789 (YX08 FWH), one of many Alexander-bodied Volvo B9TL double-deck buses in the fleet, though this one had started out with Finglands in Manchester. It was photographed on Boothferry Road as it approached its Goole terminus.

Similar vehicle No. 769 (YX59 FGO) had been new to EYMS in January 2010. Looking pristine in the sun, it is captured at Hull Interchange on 9 June 2021.

In June 2014, EYMS purchased four Volvo B7RLE saloons with MCV forty-nine-seat bodywork. One of that batch, No. 382 (YX14 HDU) was photographed in the new colours in Hull on 9 June 2021.

The road into and out of Hull's Interchange, opened in 2007, gives a good opportunity in the morning sunshine to photograph buses departing. On 9 June 2021, EYMS No. 380 (YX14 RXG), another Alexander Dennis Enviro E20D, is seen being pursued by a Stagecoach double-decker.

The latest version of the Alexander Dennis Enviro E20D is featured here, in the older colour scheme, at Beverley bus station on 8 June 2021. No. 506 (YY66 PGU) had entered service in January 2017.

As well as its buses, EYMS has a small and modern coaching fleet. Specially decorated for route X5, No. 81 (8225 KH) was photographed at its westerly terminus in Goole, on 10 August 2021. Originally registered YY63 OEM), it is a Caetano-bodied Volvo B9R. (Richard Simons)

The main depot of East Yorkshire Motor Services is on Anlaby Road in Hull. This scene was photographed on 26 August 1984, with Daimler Fleetline 872 and Leyland Royal Tiger/Roe Doyen No. 9 among others. (Richard Huggins)

Bridlington depot was smaller, though adequate for the job. Here it is, again on 26 August 1984, with the yard occupied by two Leyland Nationals and United Counties No. 189 (NNH 189Y), a Duple-bodied Leyland Leopard coach. (Richard Huggins)

The EYMS depot in Driffield was destined to close in 2014. Twelve years prior to then, No. 591 (N591 BRH), a Volvo Olympian with Alexander Royale bodywork, is seen departing for Scarborough.

Every large bus company has its service vehicles and EYMS was no exception. In use in the early 1970s was this fine example, photographed at Ferensway bus station in Hull. It had started out as a 1952-built Leyland Titan PD2/12 with fully fronted Roe bodywork, numbered 574 (MKH 83). After withdrawal, it was cut down to become a towing vehicle and operated on trade plates.

Brought out of Anlaby Road depot for the benefit of photographers in early 1987 is the Mobile Travel Office. This converted Bristol RELL6G/ECW, registered LFE 832H, had been new to Lincolnshire Road Car as No. 1216.

Fortunately, several former EYMS buses have been preserved, one of which is No. 674 (VKH 674). This unusual Albion Aberdonian with Park Royal bodywork had entered service in 1958 and was photographed in Hull, about to set out on the East Coast Rally, in 1980.

Although Lincolnshire Road Car Company had been operating into Goole for many years, it was not until the opening of the Humber Bridge in 1981 that regular services commenced into the city of Hull. Various destinations have been served on the south bank, though these have now consolidated into a Hull to Scunthorpe route, running at least hourly. Seen laying over in Hull around 1985 is No. 1453 (XTL 469X), a Willowbrook-bodied Leyland Leopard coach.

Arriving at its Hull terminus on a misty day in December 1992 is Road Car No. 453. This Leyland Tiger had been given a new East Lancs body and a 'cherished' registration – WVL 515. Stagecoach later took over the former Road Car operations.

The inland port town of Goole was, for many years, served by the West Riding Automobile Company, with services to and from the Pontefract area. On such a duty, arriving into Goole, is No. 629 (MHL 294F), a Roe-bodied Daimler Fleetline, photographed on 11 August 1972.

West Riding's services are now operated by Arriva and, 7 June 2021, we see VDL DB300/ Wright Gemini 2 No. 1544 (YJ61 OBU) coming along Boothferry Road as it approaches Goole town centre.

An unusual West Riding visitor to Bridlington in 1987 was No. 99 (UUP 830K). This Leyland National that had been new to Northern General had been converted to carry wheelchair passengers, with the addition of a centre doorway and lift.

Like all major cities in England, Kingston-upon-Hull was served by National Express services. On such a duty is National Travel West No. 94 (ANA 94Y). Photographed in Hull in 1983, this ECW-bodied Leyland Leopard coach will soon return to the other side of the Pennines.

The West Yorkshire Road Car Company's vehicles were a common sight on the East Yorkshire coast, both on express and private hire duties. On one of the former is No. 1405 (RHN 272F), an ex-United Bristol RELL6G/ECW dual-purpose saloon, photographed at Bridlington bus station in the summer of 1980.

Another second-hand vehicle in the West Yorkshire fleet, No. 2104 (LNU 345J) at Bridlington, circa 1979. This Bedford YRQ with Plaxton coachwork had been new to Midland General.

PROGRESS and Graham got together to form a partnership in 1921 and bought their first bus. Soon they had a couple of services out of Hull into the Holderness area, with a base at Easington. After the 1960s and prior to deregulation, the company was the only independent to run regularly into the city. At the Baker Street terminus on 22 June 1962, is ASD 706, a 1945-built Guy Arab II with 'utility' Northern Counties bodywork. It had been new to Western SMT in Scotland. (Les Flint)

At the same spot in December 1973, Connor & Graham's unusual Bedford VAL14 with a Yeates dual-doored coach body, registered 966 RVO. Barton Transport, of the Nottingham area, had purchased this in 1963. Public toilets in the middle of Baker Street was perhaps not the best great idea!

In 1974, Connor & Graham took over Embassy Coaches of Withernsea. Included in the purchase was MWT 687D, a Bedford VAM5 with forty-five-seat Duple Northern coachwork. It was photographed on stage carriage duties in Withernsea, shortly after the takeover.

TUP 188E was a bus that had passed through several hands before ending up with Connor & Graham. This Bedford VAM14 with forty-eight-seat Plaxton bus bodywork, had been new to The Eden, West Auckland. Connor & Graham bought it from Tait's of Morpeth. It was photographed outside the depot in Easington in 1978.

Another rare vehicle in the Connor & Graham fleet, GNF 12V, at its Hull terminus in the summer of 1991. It had started life as one of only twelve Park Royal-bodied Leyland Titans in the Greater Manchester fleet.

In 1993, Connor & Graham sold out to EYMS, bringing the bizarre situation of a former KHCT bus into the fleet. Seen here as EYMS No. 872 (PRH 246G), this Roe-bodied Leyland Atlantean PDR1/1 had been numbered 246 in the municipal fleet. Seen in central Hull in mid-1994.

One of the larger post-deregulation operators was Good News Travel/Humber Stagecoach, later trading as Metro. Several Leyland Nationals were used in the Hull area, including GKL 740N, which was given the fleet number 8903. Photographed in Hull, 1990, it had originally been No. 3522 with Maidstone & District.

Metro was later taken over by EYMS. Ironically, this Leyland Atlantean AN68/1R with Park Royal bodywork, PAT 947M had started life with EYMS, before sale to the independent. Upon takeover, they got it back! It was pressed back into service, still partly in Metro livery, in Hull in January 1993.

Appleby's, a Lincolnshire operator, started operations in East Yorkshire after taking over Boddy's Coaches of Bridlington. Deregulation saw stage carriage operations commence north of the Humber. Photographed on service in Flamborough in autumn 1987 was this Bedford YMT/ Plaxton coach, FRH 615T. It had been new to Boddy's in 1979.

Appleby's acquired several double-deck buses for use in Hull and Bridlington. Seen in the former, by Paragon station, is A674 HNB, photographed on a damp day in summer 2001. This vehicle, a Leyland Atlantean AN68D/1R with Northern Counties bodywork, had started life with Greater Manchester PTE in 1983. Appleby's have since ceased trading.

In the early years of the twenty-first century, London based CT Plus gained a contract to operate a Park & Ride service in Hull. A regular performer on this duty was fleet number BC056 (FJ59 UYL), a rare BMC Condor saloon. It is seen in central Hull on 19 August 2010.

Ideal Motors of Market Weighton, the name given to bus services operated by France's Motors, had a few buses for stage carriage work. One of these, registered Y161 HRN, is seen in Pockington on 18 September 2019, by which time ownership of the business had passed to York Pullman. This Wright-bodied Volvo B10BLE had been new to Burnley & Pendle. (Richard Simons)

Another post-deregulation Hull independent was Rhodes, running local services around the city. Pictured in Ferensway bus station in mid 1992 was Leyland National LPR 936P. This vehicle had been new to Hants & Dorset as a forty-nine seat saloon. Rhodes eventually sold their business to EYMS.

City Central was a company running commercial services in Hull around the beginning of the twenty-first century. In the summer of 2001, Bristol VRT/SL3/6LXB URP 946W was photographed beside Paragon station. Given fleet number 227, this ECW-bodied bus had been new to United Counties.

A more unusual vehicle in the City Central fleet was No. 219 (KKU 111W), an Alexander-bodied Dennis Dominator. The first owner of this bus had been South Yorkshire PTE. Again, the photo was taken in Hull in the summer of 2001.

City Central also painted some vehicles in a version of the old 'Corporation Transport' livery. Looking very smart in 2001 is 237 (PAZ 5360). New to West Yorkshire PTE, registered SUA 149R, it is a Leyland Atlantean AN68/1R with bodywork by Roe.

Alpha Bus & Coach did not last long in the world of local bus operation. In 2001, the company was running this ex-London Buses Leyland Titan/ECW, seen as TIL 6571. It had been new as a dual-doored vehicle, No. T917 (A917 SYE).

Alpha ceased trading in 2002, with East Midlands-based Dunn-Line taking over. Bought new for the Hull services was YX03 MWG, a forty-one-seat Plaxton-bodied Dennis Dart SLF. It was photographed in Central Hull on 11 July 2006. Dunn-Line pulled out of East Yorkshire operations soon afterwards.

Citilink was one of several other companies in Hull to operate bus services. As well as an ex-London AEC Routemasters, the firm ran this Optare City Pacer twenty-five-seat minibus, E941 WWE. It is seen in Bridlington, having taken part in the East Coast Run in summer 1988. Citilink was taken over by KHCT and remained as a low-cost subsidiary until 1992.

City Traveller ran a few stage carriage routes in Hull in the 1990s. A regular on such duties was VSM 783V. This Duple Dominant-bodied Leyland Leopard coach had been new in 1980 to County Durham operator Lockeys, where it had carried its original registration of XPT 566V. It was photographed outside Paragon station, on a service out to the university in December 1996.

Hedon Silverwing was a short-lived independent running a service into central Hull, which is where we see MTW 186P about to depart back to its home town in the spring of 1989. This Plaxton-bodied Ford R1114 had been new to an Essex operator. (Jim Sambrooks)

Amvale Ltd ran several services on the south bank of the Humber but ventured into Hull in the 1990s. An unusual bus to operate in the city was M814 EWV, a Dennis Dart with bodywork by Leicester Carriage Builders. When new, to East Sussex County Council, it had been fitted with a wheelchair lift. It was photographed beside Paragon station in Hull. (Richard Simons)

Frodingham Coaches was a business based in North Frodingham, near Driffield. Bought new by the company was this forty-seat Dennis Dart SLF with Caetano bodywork, registered T701 APX. Here it is in Driffield town centre in 2000. EYMS took over Frodingham Coaches in 2001 and this vehicle became No. 319 in that fleet. (Richard Simons)

EYMS retained the Frodingham Coaches identity for some of its activities for a few years. Wearing the white livery, inside Driffield depot in September 2002 is No. 92 (A20 EYC). It had been new to the Frodingham business as T649 JWB, a Volvo B7R with fifty-three-seat Plaxton coachwork.

Revill Bus ran a few post-deregulation services in the Hull and Beverley area and it is at the latter town's bus station that we see NEV 688M. This forty-nine-seat Leyland National had started life as No. 1731 in the Eastern National fleet in 1974. This photograph was taken in March 1989.

Pride of The Road was a Barnsley operator that expanded into running services in Hull in the 1990s. Several Leyland Nationals were used on these duties, including this ex-United Counties example. ORP 475M had been new as No. 475 to that company in 1974. The competition arrives at Ferensway bus station, Hull, in mid-1994. Pride of The Road ceased trading shortly after.

One independent with a stage carriage service that lasted into the early 1980s was Cherry Coaches of Beverley, who ran a town service to the nearby suburbs. A regular performer on the route was YAL 368, seen in the old Beverley bus station in 1975. This Metro-Cammell-bodied Leyland Tiger Cub had been new in 1958 as No. R368 in the East Midland fleet. It later passed to Eastern National before sale to Cherry Coaches.

Cherry Coaches also operated double-deck buses, mainly on schools duties. Seen in the depot yard c. 1978 is AEC Renown/Park Royal DFC 366D. It had been new to City of Oxford in 1966.

Parked outside the depot of Cherry Coaches, Beverley, sometime around the late 1970s, is UKW 46K. This Plaxton-bodied fifty-three-seat Ford R226 coach had been new to a Bradford operator, Boyes of Wyke.

Though Cherry Coaches are no longer with us, one Beverley independent remains, Acklam's Coaches. A town service and several rural routes are operated, and it is on the former route 5 to Model Farm that we see thirty-seat Optare Solo YX58 HBE departing from Beverley bus station on 8 June 2021.

Doncaster area independent Blue Line and its subsidiary Reliance ran several services in the mining villages and towns in South Yorkshire, one of which extended beyond Thorne Moorends to Rawcliffe and Goole. Until one of the spans at Rawcliffe Bridge was strengthened, passengers were obliged to alight from one bus, walk across the waterway, and then board another vehicle to continue their journeys. Seen at Rawcliffe Bridge on 29 October 1967 is FPT 205. This 1943-built Guy Arab II, with a Roe body constructed in 1953, had been new to Sunderland District. (Les Flint)

The Blue Line/Reliance businesses certainly like their Guys. One of the last ones purchased, NWT 496D, was photographed in the village of Rawcliffe, in the late 1970s.This Guy Arab V with seventy-three-seat Roe bodywork had been new to the Reliance organisation in 1966.

For the less busy journeys, Blue Line/Reliance used lightweight coaches, fitted with folding doors for stage carriage work. Another view in Rawcliffe village shows a Ford R192/Duple Dominant forty-five-seater registered PYG 403M. It is carrying Reliance fleet names.

The Blue Line empire fell into the hands of South Yorkshire PTE in 1979, who continued to run the route into Goole. It is here, in mid-1980, that No. 1673 (YKY 673T) was photographed. This Leyland Atlantean AN68A/1R, with Roe H45/29D bodywork, had been new in the previous year. Eventually, Firstbus took over, but has since ceased operating the Goole service and the stretch of Johnny Moor Long Lane between Rawcliffe and Moorends now has no service.

Some of the routes into Goole, previously operated by Lincolnshire Road Car Company, fell into the hands of Sweyne Coaches of Swinefleet. Operating in Goole in the spring of 1998 is MCW Metrorider F121 YVP. This twenty-eight-seat vehicle had been new to London Buses as MRL121.

Sweyne Coaches now mainly concentrate on private hire and schools duties. Operating one of the latter, in Goole on 7 June 2021, is PN04 XDF. This East Lancs-bodied Dennis Trident had been new to Blackpool Transport.

The North Humberside village of Newport once had a station on the former Hull & Barnsley Railway, but that closed in 1955. However, the villagers of Newport continued to be served with public transport provided by Holt of that village. The company maintained an infrequent service to Goole, which is where, sometime around 1982, GXS 621. This seventy-eight-seat Daimler Fleetline/Alexander had been new to a Scottish operator, Grahams of Paisley.

Also in Goole *c.* 1980 is 414 FOR. Originally purchased for the King Alfred fleet in Winchester, this fifty-three-seat Leyland Leopard, bodied by Willowbrook had been bought by Holt's after seeing service with Hants & Dorset. (Richard Simons)

Another operator to operate in Goole was Steve Stockdale, with a town service. Usually, smaller-sized buses were used, but an exception is shown here in the form of FSA 191V, photographed in the town in the 1990s. This forty-five-seat Ford R1014/Alexander had been new to Northern Scottish. (Jim Sambrooks)

Also in the Steve Stockdale fleet was JUG 352N, seen on the Goole town service in August 1998. A Bristol LHS6L with ECW B27F bodywork, it was ideal for this duty. New to West Yorkshire PTE in 1975, it later passed to Merseyside PTE and is seen still in the colours of its last operator, Brewer's of Caerau, South Wales. Steve Stockdale also ran services in Selby, but is now no longer trading.

York Pullman, based in the county's capital, ran services into what is now East Yorkshire. One such place is Stamford Bridge, famous for the lesser-known battle of 1066. Photographed here in the mid-1970s is No. 91 (UDN 491H), a fifty-two-seat Plaxton-bodied AEC Swift.

Holme-on-Spalding-Moor is also in East Yorkshire and is where York Pullman 127 (YBT 198V) is seen some time around 1984. This Bedford YMT, with Duple Dominant B63F bodywork, had been new to the company in 1980.

The village of Bubwith is now within East Yorkshire and was the home of Thornes Coaches, founded in 1949. Over the years the company has operated a wide variety of vehicles, many of which were left in the yard behind the depot after withdrawal. One such was OKP 980, a rare Beadle-Leyland, bodied by Beadle, new to Maidstone & District in 1952. It was photographed in the yard in 1975 but has since been restored and is today operated by Thornes as part of its heritage fleet.

Another unusual bus in the Thornes' fleet was MBO 1F, seen outside the depot in 1978. This Bristol LHS6L, constructed in 1968 for Western Welsh, had been fitted with a thirty-seat Weymann body that had originally been carried on an Albion Nimbus chassis. The company has since moved its base to Hemingborough, North Yorkshire, but still operates infrequent bus services into Goole and Holme-on-Spalding-Moor.

Phillips was a small operator based in the village of Shiptonthorpe, near Market Weighton. The company mainly operated contract work using an amazing variety of vehicles, which could often be seen parked up at various roadside locations in East Yorkshire. In addition, the former Hull & Barnsley Railway station yard at Howden was used and that is where four buses of the fleet were photographed in 1978. Starting on the left, these had been new to York Pullman, West Yorkshire Road Car, Trent Motor Traction and Southern National.

Phillips' FRX 162K was found outside the Shiptonthorpe headquarters in the late 1970s. This unusual Strachans-bodied Bedford YRQ had been new to the Atomic Weapons Establishment at Aldermaston, Berkshire, who had bought it for staff transport. Phillips had ceased trading by the early 1990s.

A Goole area operator that did not indulge in stage carriage operations was Advance Coaches. On a snowy day in 1975, HRO 510C was found in the company's yard. New to a Hertfordshire company, it was a Bedford VAL14 with rare Harrington Legionnaire coachwork, built to accommodate fifty-three seated passengers.

Hanson carried out contracting work in the Goole area and, quite often, one or two of the company's buses could be found in Goole railway station yard. That is where 2739 VX was photographed sometime around 1981. This Bristol MW5G with ECW bodywork had been new to Eastern National in 1961 when it was fitted with forty-one dual-purpose seats.